GW00854943

50+ Greatest Classics for Clarinet

Over 50 Favourite Melodies from the world's greatest composers arranged especially for Clarinet starting with the easiest

Amanda Oosthuizen

Jemima Oosthuizen

The Catchy Clarinet Series
Wild Music Publications

We hope you enjoy *50+ Greatest Classics for Clarinet*

Take a look at other exciting books in the series
Including: *The Catchy Clarinet book of Christmas Carols,
Christmas Duets for Tubas, The Catchy Clarinet Christmas
Bonanza, Moonlight and Roses, Chocolate and Champagne,
Easy Tunes from Around the World,* and more solos and
duets.

For more information on other amazing books please go to:
http://WildMusicPublications.com

For more **fun clarinet stuff** for **free,** visit:

http://WildMusicPublications.com/553secret-tracks65-clarinet754/

And use the password: **m@DWinds4U**

Happy Music-Making!

The Wild Music Publications Team

To keep up –to-date with our new releases, why not
follow us on Twitter

@WMPublications

Information

Tempo Markings

Adagio – slow and stately
Adagio lamentoso – slowly and sadly
Alla Marcia – like a march
Allegretto – moderately fast
Allegretto pomposo – fast and pompous
Allegro – fast and bright
Allegro assai – very fast
Allegro grazioso – fast and gracefully
Allegro maestoso – fast and majestically
Allegro vivace – fast and lively
Andante –at walking speed
Andante maestoso – a majestic walk
Andante moderato – a moderately fast
Andante non troppo – Not too fast
Andantino – slightly faster (or sometimes slower) than Andante
Andantino ingueno – not fast but with innocence
Lento - slowly
Maestoso - majestically
Moderato - moderately
Moderato con moto – moderately with movement
Molto allegro – very fast
Molto maestoso – very majestically
Presto – extremely fast
Tempo di mazurka – In the time of a mazurka - lively
Tempo di valse – In the time of a waltz
Vivace – lively and fast
Vivo - lively

Tempo Changes

rall. – *rallentando* – gradually slowing down
rit. – *ritenuto* – slightly slower

fermata – pause on this note

Dynamic Markings

dim. – *diminuendo* – gradually softer
cresc. – *crescendo* – gradually louder
cresc. poco a poco al fine – gradually louder towards the end

pp – *pianissiomo* – very softly
p – *piano* – softly
mp – *mezzo piano* – moderately soft
mf – *mezzo forte* – moderately loud
f – *forte* – loud
ff – *fortissimo* – very loud

 gradually louder
 gradually softer

Repeats

D.C. al Coda – return to the beginning and follow signs to Coda ⊕
D.C. al Fine – return to the beginning and play to *Fine*

| 1. | |
| 2. | | A repeated passage is to be played with a different ending.

Articulation

staccato – short and detached
sempre staccato – play staccato throughout

accent – played with attack

tenuto – held– pressured accent

marcato – forcefully

Ornaments

trill – rapid movement to the note above and back or from the note above in Mozart and earlier music.

mordent – three rapid notes – the principal note, the note above and the principal.

acciaccatura – a very quick note

appoggiatura – divide the main note equally between the two notes.

Contents

Ode to Joy

from *Symphony No. 9*

Ludvig van Beethoven
(1770-1827)

Spring

from *The Four Seasons*

Antonio Vivaldi
(1678-1741)

The Blue Danube

Johann Strauss
(1825-1899)

Slavonic Dance No. 1

Antonín Dvořák
(1841-1904)

4

Polovtsian Dance
from *Prince Igor*

Alexander Borodin
(1833-1887)

Andante

1

6

11

Grand Waltz
Opus 18

Frédéric Chopin
(1810-1849)

5

Voi Che Sapete

from *The Marriage of Figaro*

Wolfgang Amadeus Mozart
(1756-1791)

Bridal March

from *Lohengrin*

Richard Wagner
(1813-1883)

Ave Verum Corpus

Wolfgang Amadeus Mozart
(1756-1791)

Hornpipe
from *Water Music*

George Frideric Handel
(1685-1759)

Dido's Lament - When I am Laid to Earth
from *Dido and Aeneas*

Henry Purcell
(1659-1695)

Allegro
from *Eine Kleine Nachtmusik*

Wolfgang Amadeus Mozart
(1756-1791)

Grand March
from *Aïda*

Giuseppe Verdi
(1813-1901)

Radetzky March

Johann Strauss
(1825-1899)

Alla marcia

March

from William Tell Overture

Gioacchino Rossini
(1792-1868)

Allegro vivace

10

Adagio
from *Clarinet Concerto*

Wolfgang Amadeus Mozart
(1756-1791)

The Sorcerer's Apprentice

Paul Dukas
(1865-1935)

Brindisi

from *La Traviata*

Giuseppe Verdi
(1813-1901)

Pavane

Gabriel Fauré
(1845-1924)

Toreador's Song
from *Carmen*

Georges Bizet
(1838-1875)

Habanera
from *Carmen*

Georges Bizet
(1838-1875)

Morning

from *Peer Gynt Suite No.1*

Edvard Grieg
(1843-1907)

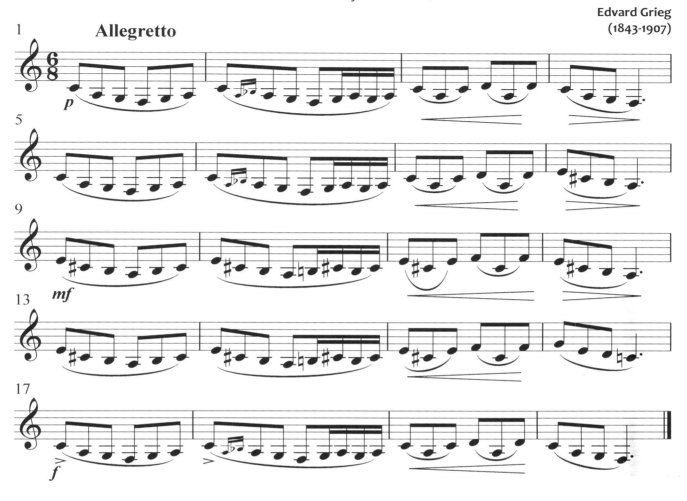

The Elephant

from *Carnival of the Animals*

Camille Saint-Saëns
(1835-1921)

14

Jupiter
from *The Planets*

Gustav Holst
(1874-1934)

Swan Theme
from *Swan Lake*

Pyotr Ilyich Tchaikovsky
(1840-1893)

La Donna è Mobile

from Rigoletto

Giussepe Verdi
(1813-1901)

Allegretto

O Mio Babbino Caro

from Gianni Schicchi

Giacomo Puccini
(1858-1924)

Andantino ingueno

Waltz

from *Die Fledermaus*

Johann Strauss
(1825-1899)

March

from *The Nutcracker Suite*

Pyotr Ilyich Tchaikovsky
(1840-1893)

Land of Hope and Glory
from *Pomp and Circumstance*

Edward Elgar
(1857-1934)

Waltz of the Flowers
from *The Nutcracker Suite*

Pyotr Ilyich Tchaikovsky
(1840-1893)

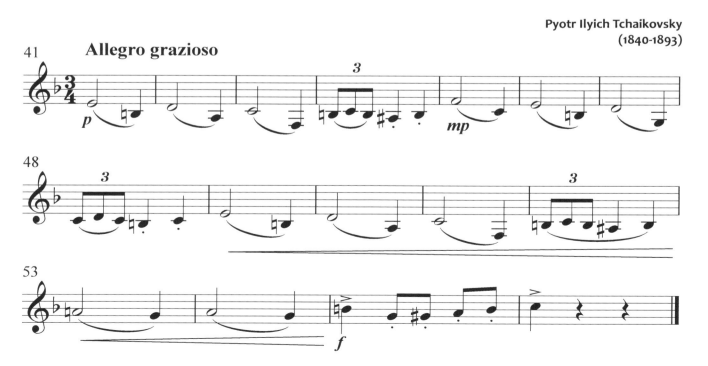

Mazurka

from *Coppelia*

Léo Delibes
(1836-1891)

Tempo di mazurka

Emperor Waltz

Johann Strauss
(1825-1899)

Tempo di valse

Dance of the Sugar Plum Fairy

from *The Nutcracker Suite*

Pyotr Ilyich Tchaikovsky
(1840-1893)

Rondo

from *The Moor's Revenge*

Henry Purcell
(1659-1695)

Nimrod

from *Enigma Variations*

Edward Elgar
(1857-1934)

Dance of the Hours

from *La Gioconda*

Amilcare Ponchielli
(1834-1886)

The Swan

from *Carnival of the Animals*

Camille Saint-Saëns
(1835-1921)

22

Anitra's Dance
from *Peer Gynt*

Edvard Grieg
(1843-1907)

Ride of the Valkyries
from *Die Walküre*

Richard Wagner
(1813-1883)

Ave Maria

Méditation sur le Premier Prélude de Piano de J.S. Bach

Charles Gounod
(1818-1893)

Valse Lente

from *Coppelia*

Léo Delibes
(1836-1891)

Waltz

from *Sleeping Beauty*

Pyotr Ilyich Tchaikovsky
(1840-1893)

24

Pizzicato Polka

Berceuse

from *Dolly Suite*

Hallelujah Chorus
from *Messiah*

George Frideric Handel
(1685-1759)

Galop and Can-Can
from *Orpheus in the Underworld*

Jacques Offenbach
(1819-1880)

Flower Duet

from *Lakmé*

Léo Delibes
(1836-1891)

Jesu, Joy of Man's Desiring

Johann Sebastian Bach
(1685-1750)

In the Hall of the Mountain King

from *Peer Gynt*

Edvard Grieg
(1843-1907)

1 **Alla marcia**

pp   *sempre staccato*

5

cresc. poco a poco al fine

9

13

17

21

The Queen of the Night Aria

from *The Magic Flute*

Wolfgang Amadeus Mozart
(1756-1791)

Finale

from *Carnival of the Animals*

Camille Saint-Saëns
(1835-1921)

Molto allegro

If you have enjoyed **50+ Greatest Classics for Clarinet,** why not try the other books in the **Catchy Clarinet** series!

For more info, please visit: **WildMusicPublications.com**

All of our books are available to download, or you can order from Amazon.

Introducing:

Fish 'n' Ships

Clarinet Music Practice Notebook

Christmas Carols

Trick or Treat – A Halloween Suite

Very Easy Christmas Duets for Teacher and Pupil

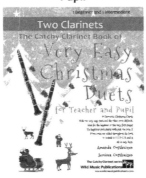

Champagne and Chocolate

Clarinet Music Theory Book 1

Christmas Duets

Easy Duets from Around the World

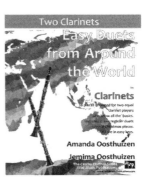

11073921R00021

Printed in Great Britain
by Amazon